Dating Website Predators
Are After Your Money

I AM NOT YOUR ATM CARD

SHEN BECK

First published 2026

THANK YOU

I would like to express my sincere appreciation to **Basma** and **Joe** for their continuous support, encouragement, and confidence in this work.

Your understanding and support during challenging times have been invaluable.

I am truly grateful for your trust and for being an important part of this journey.

TABLE OF CONTENTS

ABOUT THE AUTHOR

I am the author of this booklet, which is based on years of personal experience, research, and exploration of dating and chatting websites while searching for a sincere relationship that could eventually lead to marriage.

Like many others, I entered these platforms with hope, curiosity, and genuine intentions. During this journey, I interacted with many different types of dating websites, communicated with people from different backgrounds, and spent significant amounts of money trying to build meaningful connections. Some conversations appeared honest and promising at first, while others slowly revealed hidden intentions, emotional manipulation, and financial exploitation.

There were moments when a simple message notification created excitement and hope. A profile photo, a kind conversation, or a shared interest could make someone feel that a real connection was finally beginning. But sometimes, behind those conversations were people hiding completely different motives.

Through this booklet, I want to share the real experiences and situations I personally encountered, so that others can avoid the same mistakes. These stories are not generated by artificial intelligence or created for entertainment alone; they are inspired by genuine experiences, observations, and patterns that repeatedly appear in the world of online dating platforms.

My goal is not to discourage anyone from seeking relationships online. Genuine people still exist, and meaningful relationships can happen. However, awareness, patience, and emotional control are essential in a digital world where appearances can often be misleading.

Inside these pages, you will discover different types of scams, emotional manipulation tactics, warning signs, and practical advice that may help you protect your time, emotions, personal information, and finances. More importantly, you will see how easily loneliness, hope, curiosity, and emotional attachment can sometimes cloud judgment.

I hope this booklet helps you stay cautious without losing hope, aware without becoming fearful, and wiser while navigating the complex world of online relationships.

Thank you for taking the time to read this work, and I hope you find it both useful and eye-opening.

INTRODUCTION

Dating sites and social platforms have made it easier than ever for strangers from different parts of the world to meet and connect. Every day, thousands of people join these platforms searching for friendship, companionship, love, or even marriage. Some discover genuine relationships that change their lives for the better. Others, however, unknowingly step into a world of deception, manipulation, emotional games, and financial exploitation.

A few years ago, I received a message from someone whose profile appeared completely genuine. The photos looked real, the conversation felt natural, and the attention seemed sincere. At first, I felt optimistic and excited about where the connection might lead. But slowly, subtle warning signs began to appear. The conversations shifted from simple introductions to emotional stories, financial struggles, and disguised requests for help.

What started as an ordinary online conversation eventually became a lesson about how easily trust can be manipulated in digital spaces.

Later, I encountered other experiences—some suspicious, some emotionally confusing, and some surprisingly genuine. Over time, I began noticing recurring patterns, repeated tactics, and psychological methods used by people whose real intentions had nothing to do with love or relationships.

This booklet was written to help readers recognize those patterns before becoming emotionally or financially trapped. Rather than focusing on specific countries or platforms, these pages explore the many differentways people can be manipulated online through false affection, emotional pressure, fake emergencies, investment schemes, and carefully crafted lies.

The stories and situations ahead may sometimes seem shocking, strange, or even unbelievable, yet many of them begin with something as simple as a friendly message, a compliment, or a late-night conversation.

While online dating can create meaningful opportunities, it also requires caution, patience, emotional awareness, and good judgment. Your choices, boundaries, and decisions ultimately shape your experience.

This guide is designed to help you:

- Recognize common warning signs.
- Protect your personal information and finances.
- Avoid emotional manipulation and financial scams.
- Navigate dating platforms more safely and confidently.

As you continue reading, you will discover real scenarios, practical advice, and lessons learned through experience—lessons that may help you avoid costly emotional and financial mistakes in the future.

Remember: Not every smiling profile is honest, not every emotional story is real, and not every connection is built on sincere intentions.

SECTION 1: TYPES OF DATING SITES

In this section, I will share the types of websites I used and how I categorized them during my research to understand how they function. I will discuss the user experience on these platforms, how communication typically takes place, and the features and services offered—many of which appear repeatedly across different sites. I will also touch upon the costs involved. While the platforms may appear similar at first glance, differences in pricing models, features, and user experience often depend on regions, nationalities, or platform-specific strategies.

1. Subscription-Based Sites (Membership Tiers)

In this type of platform, after registering, completing your profile, and confirming your email, users are presented with several membership tiers—usually three or more—displayed in a comparison table. This table outlines the features included in each tier, along with their respective prices.

Once a plan is selected, payment is typically charged on a monthly basis.

Key services often include:

- Chat translation
- Customer support assistance
- Viewing who visited your profile or added you to their "Favorites"
- Sending messages and boosting profile visibility in search results

After subscribing, a badge is usually displayed on your profile, indicating your membership level. Upgrading to a higher tier is often possible by paying the difference, while downgrading typically requires contacting customer support, depending on platform policies.

Prices are generally high and can easily exceed $100 to $200 per month. Some platforms even offer personal consultants who help filter and recommend profiles based on user preferences—an additional paid service separate from the subscription.

2. Credit-Based or Coin-Based Sites

After creating an account with basic details such as age, name, goals, and email—and verifying your email (which may sometimes land in the spam folder)—users are directed to a page displaying profile photos of potential matches.

At this stage, a promotional offer is often presented, encouraging users to purchase credits at a discounted rate to begin interaction.

The platform typically explains that these credits are required for messaging or video calls, with costs calculated per message or per minute of conversation.

Even before any payment is made, users may begin receiving engaging or provocative messages such as:

- “What do you like?”
- “Do you think I’m beautiful?”
- “Would you like to travel with me?”

These messages are designed to trigger curiosity and encourage users to respond, which ultimately leads to purchasing credits.

It is also important to note that translation services—if available—may require a separate subscription in addition to credit usage for communication.

Users may occasionally earn small bonus credits through profile completion or daily activity.

Personal Warning

Based on personal experience, this model can become significantly more expensive than subscription-based sites if spending is not carefully controlled. In some cases, users may spend over $1,000 without meaningful results, as credits are quickly consumed through messaging or video calls.

3. Classic Dating Sites

I call these "classic" dating sites because of their simplicity. Unlike subscription-heavy platforms or credit-based systems, these sites focus on straightforward communication without overwhelming users with multiple pricing structures or complicated features.

Getting started is usually simple: register with an email address, complete your profile, upload a photo, and begin browsing. The interface is generally user-friendly, making these platforms particularly appealing for those who prefer a more traditional online dating experience.

Communication primarily takes place through an internal messaging system. You may receive notifications that someone has sent you a message, but the content is often blurred or partially hidden until one or both users have an active subscription. While free members can usually browse profiles and send limited messages, meaningful communication often requires a paid membership.

Subscribing typically allows you to:

- Read and reply to messages without restrictions.
- Remove advertisements.
- Access advanced search filters.
- See additional profile details.
- Improve your overall communication experience on the platform.

Before purchasing any membership, here is some valuable information that can save you both money and frustration:

- Most sites display badges or icons indicating whether another member has an active subscription. If both parties are subscribers, communication is generally much smoother, as messages are visible without restrictions.
- Membership plans are usually available in different durations, such as one month, three months, six months, or one year. In many cases, the basic membership level is sufficient for normal browsing and communication.
- Translation services are often not included and may require separate payment if you are communicating with someone who does not speak your language.
- Optional features such as virtual gifts, roses, stickers, profile boosts, and highlighted profiles frequently require additional coins or credits, even when you already have a subscription.
- From a cost perspective, these platforms are often the most economical option. A three-month or yearly subscription can cost less than a single month on some premium subscription sites or a short period of active messaging on credit-based platforms.

For users seeking a straightforward dating experience without constantly monitoring credits or paying for every interaction, classic dating sites are often the simplest and most budget-friendly choice.

SECTION 2: TYPES OF PEOPLE ON DATING PLATFORMS

Dating platforms bring together different types of people, each with different intentions and expectations.

- People who join dating platforms primarily out of curiosity, boredom, or simply to pass the time, without any genuine intention of building a serious relationship.
- People who use these platforms for manipulation, blackmail, scams, or financial extortion.
- People who create false identities and lie about nearly every aspect of their lives, including their appearance, relationship status, profession, age, or personal circumstances.
- People who are mainly present for entertainment, attention, emotional validation, or personal gain rather than sincere emotional connection.

- People searching for a "sugar daddy" or "sugar mama" relationship, where financial support and gifts are expected in exchange for attention, companionship, or affection.
- Honest and genuine people—although they are less common—do exist on these platforms.

Real users usually display clear and consistent signs of sincerity. They engage in meaningful conversations instead of relying only on flirtation, repetitive compliments, or intrusive personal questions. They respect boundaries, avoid rushing emotional attachment, and allow trust to develop naturally over time. Genuine people also tend to share personal details gradually and feel comfortable with mutual openness rather than one-sided emotional investment. Most importantly, their behavior remains consistent over time, which is often one of the strongest indicators of honesty and authenticity.

SECTION 3: TYPES OF RELATIONSHIPS ON THESE PLATFORMS

People join dating sites for many different reasons, and one of the biggest mistakes newcomers make is assuming everyone is looking for the same thing. Some people are simply looking for friendship and someone with whom they can share their thoughts after a long day. They may enjoy meaningful conversations, exchanging life experiences, or building a connection without any immediate romantic expectations.

Others are seeking short-term or long-term relationships. Some want companionship and excitement in the present, while others are carefully exploring whether a deeper connection could develop over time. Their goals may evolve as they get to know someone better.

There are also individuals who are genuinely interested in learning about different cultures, traditions, and ways of life. They enjoy meeting people from other countries, practicing new languages, and broadening their understanding of the world through personal connections.

For others, marriage is the primary objective from the very beginning. They join these platforms with a clear intention: to find a compatible life partner rather than engage in casual conversations or temporary relationships. These users often approach communication more seriously and tend to ask practical questions earlier in the process.

Understanding these different motivations is important because it helps set realistic expectations. A person seeking friendship may communicate very differently from someone actively searching for a spouse, and recognizing those differences early can save both time and disappointment.

SECTION 4: GENERAL TIPS AND PRACTICAL ADVICE

Essential Safety and Practical Tips Before You Begin

Before creating your first dating profile, remember that online dating is not just about meeting people—it is also about protecting your privacy, managing your expectations, and avoiding unnecessary risks. The following guidelines are based on observations, personal experiences, and common situations encountered across many dating platforms.

Protect Your Identity

Create a separate email address exclusively for dating platforms. This keeps your main accounts private and reduces risk.

Most platforms require subscriptions, even if they appear free. Be aware that some may collect or share user data, so always read their privacy notices and warnings carefully.

Profile and Verification Safety

- Avoid uploading personal photos immediately unless necessary.
- Never trust profile pictures blindly—verify them using image search if possible.
- Cross-check details like age, location, and background if anything feels inconsistent.
- Be cautious if the same images or profiles appear across multiple platforms.

Communication Caution

- Be careful when someone asks for sensitive details early (income, address, lifestyle).
- Avoid sharing personal social media accounts at the beginning.
- Some platforms monitor messages, and sharing external contact details may lead to restrictions.
- If someone repeatedly asks the same questions or avoids details, treat it as a warning sign.

Financial Awareness

- Never send money in early conversations under any circumstance.
- Be cautious of users who frequently discuss financial matters or hint at money.
- Avoid paying immediately for contact features—check if free features or trials exist first.
- Use backup payment methods (prepaid cards or limited funds) instead of main accounts.
- Disable auto-renewal after subscribing to avoid unexpected charges.

Platform Behavior

- Log in regularly at first to evaluate activity before committing to a subscription.
- Some sites send frequent notifications or messages to encourage payments—be aware of this.
- If dissatisfied, delete or deactivate your account instead of keeping it inactive.

- Avoid inactive or suspicious platforms, even if profiles look appealing.

Emotional Awareness

- Take your time in the "getting to know" stage before forming emotional attachments.
- Early feelings of attraction are common but should not be mistaken for love.
- If something feels "too perfect," it often isn't genuine.
- Real relationships develop gradually, not instantly.

Scam Indicators

- Be cautious of users who quickly request personal contact or financial discussions.
- Check email addresses for unusual formats or suspicious patterns.
- Verify that WhatsApp or contact numbers match claimed country details.

- If someone reappears only after your subscription expires, avoid renewing just for them.
- Repeated blocking, sudden disappearance, or inconsistent behavior can indicate fake profiles.

Final Reminder

Stay patient and observant. Genuine intentions become clearer over time, not in the first interaction.

STORY INTRODUCTION

These warnings are not theoretical; they are real situations that can begin with a very ordinary moment.

I stood in my kitchen, sipping the last warm drops of my morning coffee, when my phone vibrated with a notification. It was a direct message from an online match. We had never spoken before, yet here it was—a message filled with desperation, wrapped in the alluring simplicity of casual conversation.

"Hi," the message read. "I know this may sound strange, but I feel like I can talk to you."

At first, there was nothing unusual about it. Dating sites are full of people trying to start conversations, and many open with awkward or overly personal messages. I almost ignored it.

Instead, I replied with a simple greeting.

Within minutes, another message arrived. Then another. Soon, the conversation flowed effortlessly. She seemed attentive, asked thoughtful questions, and appeared genuinely interested in my life. Unlike many people on dating platforms who disappear after a few exchanges, she always responded quickly.

Over the next few days, she shared pieces of her story. She spoke about loneliness, difficult relationships, and the challenges she faced in daily life. Some details were vague, but at the time, that did not seem important. What stood out was how easily she created a sense of familiarity.

That is often how these situations begin.

Not with a request for money.

Not with a dramatic emergency.

Not with obvious warning signs.

They begin with trust.

The person learns your routine. They discover when you wake up, when you go to work, and when you are most likely to be online. They remember small details from previous conversations and use them to create the impression of a genuine connection.

As the days pass, your guard slowly lowers.

You stop analyzing.

You stop verifying.

You begin believing.

And that is precisely the moment when many scams truly begin.

The request rarely comes immediately. Sometimes it takes days. Sometimes weeks. In some cases, scammers invest months building a relationship before revealing their real objective. By then, the victim is no longer speaking to a stranger. They believe they are speaking to someone they know, trust, and care about.

What happened next in this conversation followed a pattern I would encounter many times over the years—a pattern that has cost countless people their money, their confidence, and occasionally even their hope of finding a genuine relationship.

FIRST STORY: ONLINE BEGGING

The conversation began like many others.

A few messages were exchanged about hobbies, work, and daily life. She seemed friendly, polite, and genuinely interested in getting to know me. Nothing about the interaction raised any immediate concerns.

A few days later, the tone of the conversation changed.

She mentioned that she was worried and having difficulty concentrating. Naturally, I asked what was wrong.

At first, she hesitated. Then came a long message explaining that she was facing financial hardship. According to her story, she was a university student struggling to pay tuition fees. She spoke about her dreams, her determination to succeed, and how close she was to losing everything because she could not make the next payment.

The amount she requested was relatively small.

"Just enough to help me get through this difficult period," she wrote.

When I did not immediately offer assistance, more details followed. She described sleepless nights, mounting pressure, and fears about her future. The story was emotional, carefully presented, and designed to trigger sympathy.

Over the years, I would encounter many similar situations. The details changed, but the pattern remained remarkably consistent.

In this type of scam, the person begins by sharing financial problems and emotional hardships, hoping to gain your trust and compassion before asking for money. This tactic relies on what psychologists often call a "sympathy trigger"—an attempt to influence decisions by appealing to emotions rather than facts.

Common scenarios include:

- Claiming to be a university student struggling to pay tuition fees and asking for financial assistance.
- Pretending to be a mother who cannot afford food or necessities for her children.
- Saying she has been surviving on water alone for days due to a natural disaster, severe weather, or economic hardship.
- Claiming that rent is overdue and that eviction is imminent unless someone helps.
- Describing a sudden medical emergency that supposedly requires immediate financial support.

These stories are often highly emotional, but they typically lack independent evidence that can verify their authenticity.

How Should You Respond?

- Never reveal your salary, savings, or overall financial situation.
- Respond politely but firmly. For example: "I have many financial obligations of my own" or

"I am dealing with personal challenges at the moment."

- Avoid feeling guilty for refusing financial requests from someone you barely know.
- If the conversation becomes focused on money rather than building a relationship, treat it as a warning sign.
- If the pressure continues, end the conversation immediately—even if the person blocks you, becomes upset, or attempts to make you feel responsible for their situation.

Lesson Learned

Genuine relationships are built on trust, communication, and shared experiences—not financial assistance. When someone you've barely met begins asking for money, it is often a sign that the conversation was never truly about connection in the first place.

SECOND STORY: ENTERTAINMENT

Unlike many people on dating sites, she did not immediately overwhelm me with attention. In fact, she seemed slightly reserved. Her replies were short, and sometimes hours passed before she responded. That made her appear more genuine.

After several days of messaging through the dating platform, she suggested moving the conversation elsewhere.

“These sites are annoying,” she wrote. “Do you have WhatsApp or email?”

The request seemed reasonable. After all, many people prefer communicating outside dating platforms. Without thinking much about it, I shared my contact information.

Once we moved off the site, the conversation became more personal. She sent photos from her daily life, talked about her interests, and asked questions about mine. She seemed interested in building a connection rather than rushing anything.

A week later, she sent another message. "I have something special I'd like to share with you."

Naturally, curiosity took over.

She hinted at private photos and exclusive content that she did not share with everyone. There was no direct mention of money at first. Instead, she focused on creating anticipation and making me feel chosen.

Then came the catch.

She explained that sending the content required a small payment. According to her, it was only fair because of the time and effort involved. The amount was not particularly large, which made it easier to justify.

I hesitated.

She reassured me. "It's only once."

"It's not much."

"You seem like a trustworthy person."

Eventually, the payment was sent.

Shortly afterward, several photos arrived. But something felt off. The images looked professional, almost as if they had been taken from somewhere else. There was no way to verify whether they actually belonged to the person I had been talking to.

A few days later, another offer appeared. This time there were additional photos. Then another request. Then another.

Each interaction came with a new price.

What began as a conversation gradually transformed into a transaction.

The connection I thought I was building turned out to be a sales process.

Over the years, I noticed the same pattern repeatedly. The objective was rarely friendship or a relationship. Instead, the goal was to create enough emotional interest and curiosity that sending money felt like a natural next step.

In some cases, the person may provide photos or videos after receiving payment. In others, excuses begin immediately. They may claim the payment never arrived, that additional fees are required, or that technical issues prevented them from sending what was promised.

The details vary, but the strategy remains remarkably similar: establish trust first, introduce exclusivity second, and request money third.

How Should You Respond?

- Avoid sharing personal contact information too quickly.
- Be cautious when conversations move from relationship-building to financial transactions.
- Remember that photos, videos, and promises can easily be obtained from other sources and may not belong to the person you're speaking with.
- Never assume that paying once will be the last request. In many cases, it becomes the beginning of a cycle of repeated demands.

- If the conversation becomes centered on payments rather than genuine communication, step away immediately.

Lesson Learned

A genuine connection does not require purchasing attention. When financial requests become part of getting to know someone, it is often a sign that the relationship itself is no longer the product—the relationship has become the sales pitch.

THIRD STORY: **THE FAKE PHISHING WEBSITE (E-COMMERCE SETUP)**

It began in a way that felt completely harmless.

A man matched with a woman on a dating app who introduced herself as an entrepreneur running a successful online fashion boutique. She spoke confidently about her work—branding, customer experience, online sales, and expanding her business. Their conversations quickly moved beyond casual chatting and turned into discussions about ambition, goals, and building something meaningful.

For weeks, the connection felt natural. There was no pressure. No requests for money. Only shared interest in entrepreneurship and steady emotional bonding.

Then one day, she shared something new. She said she was redesigning her online store and wanted his opinion on the new layout.

It felt flattering—like his input mattered to her work.

She sent a link. The page looked professional. Clean branding, modern design, product listings, and familiar e-commerce styling made it appear legitimate. Nothing immediately suggested danger.

When he clicked the link, a pop-up appeared. It asked him to log in to verify his identity and confirm his age before accessing the store. The message looked routine, almost like standard compliance for online shopping platforms. It requested email credentials first, then redirected him to what appeared to be a bank verification step.

Everything looked normal enough to avoid suspicion.

But it was not a store. It was a phishing setup. The login forms were fake interfaces designed to capture sensitive credentials. The moment he entered his details, the information was transmitted to attackers in real time.

Within hours, the consequences became clear. He was locked out of his accounts. Unauthorized transactions began appearing.

Access to his primary bank accounts had been compromised, and funds were being drained rapidly before he could respond.

The woman who had shared the "store design" disappeared from the platform.

The boutique, the link, and the relationship were all part of the same structure—built not to sell fashion, but to harvest trust.

How Should You Respond?

- Never log in to banking or email accounts through links sent by individuals met online.
- Be cautious of "feedback requests" that involve account access or verification steps.
- Always access financial or email services directly through official websites or apps.
- Avoid entering credentials into unfamiliar pages, even if they look professional.

- Treat unexpected pop-ups requesting sensitive data as potential phishing attempts.
- If credentials are entered by mistake, immediately change passwords and contact your bank.

Lesson Learned

Modern scams often disguise themselves as professional opportunities or shared interests.

In this case, trust was built through conversation, not requests—making the final trap harder to detect.

FOURTH STORY: FINANCIAL BLACKMAIL

This is one of the most dangerous and emotionally damaging scams discussed in this guide because it can quickly escalate into fear, panic, humiliation, and psychological pressure.

Here is how the situation usually develops: After spending some time talking on a dating platform, the other person suggests moving the conversation to a more personal application such as WhatsApp, Facebook, Telegram, or another private messaging service. At first, everything may seem normal and harmless. The conversations become friendlier, more personal, and sometimes flirtatious in order to build trust and emotional comfort.

Soon afterward, the person insists on having a private video call. During the conversation, they may first appear relaxed, charming, and emotionally interested in you. They often make sure you are completely alone and comfortable before gradually steering the interaction in a more intimate direction.

Then, the manipulation begins.

The person may start undressing, acting seductively, or encouraging you to do the same. In that moment, many people lower their guard because they believe the interaction is private and genuine. However, what you may not notice is that the video call is often being secretly recorded. Sometimes, the scammer may appear distracted, press unusual buttons, adjust the screen repeatedly, or manipulate the camera angle while recording everything happening during the call.

Once the conversation ends, the situation suddenly changes.

The scammer begins threatening you with the recorded footage. They may demand money immediately while claiming they will upload the video to social media platforms, YouTube, or adult websites. In some cases, they may threaten to send the footage to your family members, friends, employer, or social media contacts. Others may use edited screenshots, fake images, or fabricated messages to increase fear and emotional pressure.

This type of scam is especially dangerous because it targets emotions rather than just money.

Victims often panic, feel ashamed, or fear public embarrassment, which leads them to make rushed decisions. Unfortunately, **paying the scammer rarely solves the problem**. In many cases, once payment is sent, the blackmailer continues demanding more money repeatedly.

How Should You Respond?

If the conversation suddenly becomes overly sexual or the other person pressures you to undress during a video call, end the call immediately.

Do not allow emotional excitement, curiosity, or pressure to override your judgment. Even if you have already partially participated in the conversation, stop immediately and disconnect the call.

Afterward:

- Block the person on all communication platforms.

- Do not continue negotiating or responding to threats.
- Avoid sending money under pressure or fear.
- Save screenshots or evidence if necessary.
- Strengthen your privacy settings on social media accounts.

Most importantly, remember that scammers rely heavily on fear and panic. Staying calm and cutting communication quickly is often the safest response.

Lesson Learned

Blackmailers succeed by creating panic. Their greatest weapon is not the recording itself—it is the fear that follows. The moment fear takes control, people stop thinking rationally. Recognizing the warning signs early and protecting your privacy is often the best defense against becoming a victim.

FIFTH STORY: THE DECEPTION

In this type of scheme, a woman sends a message to your account on a dating site regardless of whether you have an active subscription.

The message often contains flattering phrases such as:

- "Your profile really caught my attention."
- "I felt an instant connection when I saw your profile."
- "I would love to get to know you better."
- "You seem different from the other men here."

At first glance, these messages may appear genuine and personal. However, if the platform allows you to see who has viewed your profile, you may discover something interesting: The person who supposedly found your profile so appealing may never have viewed it at all.

This raises an obvious question: How can someone be deeply interested in your profile if they have never taken the time to read it?

In many cases, the purpose of these messages is not to start a meaningful conversation. Instead, they are designed to create curiosity and encourage users to purchase a subscription so they can read, unlock, or respond to the message.

The strategy is simple but effective. The message creates the impression that an attractive opportunity is waiting just beyond the paywall. Excitement and curiosity often lead users to subscribe before they have had time to evaluate whether the profile is genuine.

It is important to remember that a flattering message is not proof of genuine interest. Sometimes it is simply a marketing tool intended to increase subscriptions and engagement on the platform.

How Should You Respond?

- Do not rush to purchase a subscription simply because you received an unexpected message.

- Check whether the sender has actually viewed your profile or interacted with your account in any meaningful way.
- Wait a few days and observe whether the profile appears active and consistent.
- Look for signs of genuine engagement rather than generic compliments that could be sent to hundreds of users.
- Evaluate the overall quality of the site before spending money to unlock conversations.

Lesson Learned

Curiosity is one of the strongest motivators in online dating. Before paying to respond to a message, ask yourself whether the person's interest appears genuine—or whether the message was carefully designed to make you reach for your wallet.

SIXTH STORY: THE INVESTMENT

One of the most persuasive scams on dating platforms is the "investment opportunity" trap because it does not begin with obvious requests for money. Instead, it starts with emotional connection, trust-building, and the illusion of success.

In this type of situation, you may receive a friendly message from someone on a dating site. At first, the conversation feels completely normal. The person asks casual questions about your hobbies, daily routine, work life, and future goals. The interaction may continue for several days, sometimes even weeks, creating the impression that genuine interest and emotional connection are developing naturally.

After gaining your trust, the person asks to continue the conversation through WhatsApp, Telegram, Instagram, or another social media platform. This shift often makes the interaction feel more personal and authentic.

Gradually, the conversations become more detailed. The person starts asking questions about your financial situation—your job, salary, savings, lifestyle, or future ambitions. At first, these questions may appear harmless or part of normal curiosity between two people getting to know each other.

Then the story changes.

The person begins describing a luxurious and successful lifestyle. They may claim to own a beauty salon, a clothing business, a café, or another profitable company. Sometimes they mention expensive travel, shopping, or financial independence to appear successful and trustworthy. Eventually, they introduce the topic of investments, digital currency, Forex trading, or online financial platforms.

For example, they may say something like: "My cousin manages investments for me, and I make extra income every month."

"I started with a small amount and now I earn thousands."

"I want to help you succeed too because I care about you."

At this stage, the scam becomes psychological rather than romantic.

The victim often feels emotionally connected and begins believing that the other person genuinely wants to help improve their life. Some scammers even send screenshots of fake profits, luxury lifestyles, or fabricated bank transactions to strengthen the illusion. Others become emotionally manipulative, acting disappointed or offended if you hesitate to invest.

One of the most dangerous aspects of this scam is how persuasive and gradual it feels. A person may start believing:

"This person talks to me every day."

"She shares personal stories."

"She seems financially successful."

"Why would someone who likes me try to deceive me?"

That emotional trust is exactly what the scammer wants.

In many cases, once money is transferred into the so-called investment platform, the victim either loses access to the funds completely or is pressured to keep investing larger amounts. Some scammers even allow small fake profits at first to create confidence before convincing the victim to send much more money later.

If the victim refuses, the scammer may suddenly change personality—becoming cold, insulting, manipulative, or accusing the person of wasting their time after "trying to help."

How Should You Respond?

The moment someone on a dating platform begins heavily discussing investments, trading opportunities, cryptocurrency, or fast financial success, treat it as a major warning sign.

A genuine relationship should not quickly turn into financial advice or investment pressure.

Lessons Learned:

- Politely distance yourself from the discussion.
  • Do not share financial information, savings details, or banking data.

- Never transfer money because of emotional attachment or trust.
- Avoid clicking suspicious investment links or downloading unknown applications.
- Remember that scammers often use fake success stories and emotional manipulation to appear credible.

Most importantly, understand that real emotional connection should never depend on financial investment.

SEVENTH STORY: MOBILE CREDIT REQUEST

We had been exchanging messages for several days. The conversation was pleasant, and unlike many people on dating sites, she responded consistently. We talked about hobbies, family, work, and future goals. Gradually, the exchanges became longer and more personal.

Then one evening, just as the conversation seemed to be developing into something meaningful, she sent a message that changed the tone entirely.

"I'm sorry," she wrote. "I may disappear for a while. I don't have enough mobile data left to stay online."

At first, it sounded like a reasonable problem. After all, internet access is not equally available everywhere, and many people rely on prepaid mobile plans.

The next message arrived a few minutes later. "If you really want to keep talking to me, perhaps you could help me recharge my phone."

The amount requested was small. In fact, it seemed insignificant compared to the possibility of continuing a promising conversation. The request was presented as a practical solution rather than a demand for money.

Wanting to be helpful, some people agree. A recharge is sent. The conversation continues.

A few days later, however, the same problem suddenly returns.

"My internet package expired again."

"My phone credit is finished."

"I can't afford another recharge this week."

Before long, what appeared to be a one-time favor becomes a recurring request.

In some cases, the person may genuinely use the credit. In others, the mobile credit is sold or converted into cash, turning the conversation into a source of income. The relationship itself becomes secondary to the financial benefit.

One clue often appears after communication stops. Some dating platforms allow users to see when a member is active. You may discover that the person who supposedly lost internet access continues logging into the site regularly while claiming they cannot communicate with you.

How Should You Respond?

- Be cautious when financial requests appear early in a conversation.
- Remember that mobile credit, gift cards, and small recharges are still forms of financial assistance.
- Avoid sending money or phone credit simply to keep a conversation alive.
- Pay attention to whether the person's actions match their explanations.

- If the same problem repeatedly appears, consider it a warning sign.

Lesson Learned

One of the most effective scams is also one of the simplest. Because the requested amount is small, people often lower their guard. However, a genuine connection should not depend on repeated financial assistance. If someone consistently needs money, credit, or recharges to maintain contact, it may be a sign that the conversation serves a financial purpose rather than a personal one.

Final Thought: A person who is genuinely interested in getting to know you will usually find a way to communicate. A person who repeatedly needs your money to communicate may be interested in something entirely different.

EIGHTH STORY: BUYING A SMARTPHONE

This time, I thought I found a loyal partner. She seemed friendly and interested in getting to know me better.

However, there was one recurring problem. Sometimes she would disappear in the middle of a conversation and return hours later with an apology.

Eventually, she explained the reason. The device she was using did not belong to her.

According to her story, she was borrowing a smartphone from her sister, cousin, or another family member. Sometimes she claimed to use a shared computer at home or an internet café. Because the device was not hers, she could only communicate for short periods before losing access.

At first, the explanation sounded believable. You know when you are in active communication with someone you become interested in, you start to believe that person.

Then came the next step.

"I wish we could talk more."

"If I had my own smartphone, we could chat every day."

"We could even have video calls and get to know each other properly."

Eventually, she asked whether I could help her buy a smartphone.

The implication was clear: If I helped solve her problem, our connection would become stronger and more meaningful.

For someone emotionally invested in the conversation, the idea can be tempting. After all, the request appears practical. A smartphone would supposedly allow more communication, more video calls, and a closer relationship.

Unfortunately, this is where many people make a costly mistake.

Once the phone is purchased—or money is sent to buy one—the conversation often changes. Some people become less responsive. Others disappear entirely. In certain cases, additional requests soon follow, such as needing money for internet access, repairs, accessories, or other unexpected expenses.

The promised relationship never develops, but the financial requests continue.

How Should You Respond?

- Avoid purchasing phones, computers, tablets, or other devices for someone you have only met online.
- Be cautious when a conversation repeatedly focuses on what the other person lacks, rather than on building a genuine connection.
- Remember that requests for devices are still requests for financial assistance.
- Do not allow feelings of sympathy or hope to influence financial decisions.
- If someone continues pressuring you after you decline, consider it a significant warning sign.

Lesson Learned

A genuine relationship should not depend on expensive gifts or purchases. While owning a smartphone may make communication easier, it should never become a condition for continuing a conversation. If someone you've only recently met insists that your connection depends on buying them a device, they may be more interested in the gift than in the relationship itself.

Final Thought: Be careful of conversations that turn ordinary communication problems into financial obligations. The moment a relationship starts requiring purchases to survive, it may no longer be a relationship at all—it may be a transaction.

NINTH STORY: BUYING A CAMERA

The conversation seemed promising from the start.

After exchanging messages for several days, we eventually moved on to voice calls and discussed the possibility of video chatting. However, whenever the topic came up, she had an explanation ready.

"My camera isn't very good."

"The image is blurry."

"You probably wouldn't even recognize me."

At first, these comments appeared harmless. Many people use older devices, and poor camera quality is not unusual. In fact, the explanation sounded reasonable enough that I barely thought about it.

As the conversation continued, she returned to the subject repeatedly. She mentioned how much she wished we could have clearer video calls. She talked about how difficult it was to build trust when the camera quality was so poor. Gradually, the problem became a recurring theme in our conversations.

Then came the solution.

"If only I had a better camera."

"I would love to show you my life properly."

"We could spend so much more time together."

Eventually, the hints became a direct request. Rather than asking for a camera itself, she asked for money so she could purchase one on her own.

The request was framed as a way to strengthen the relationship. After all, who wouldn't want clearer video calls and better communication?

But this is often where caution becomes necessary.

Once money is involved, the original purpose of the conversation can become difficult to distinguish from financial motives. In some cases, the camera is never purchased. In others, additional requests soon follow for internet access, accessories, repairs, or other unexpected expenses.

And sometimes, if the request is declined, the person disappears entirely, revealing that the relationship may never have been the primary goal.

How Should You Respond?

- Be cautious when conversations repeatedly focus on a problem that can supposedly be solved with money.
- Avoid sending funds for cameras, phones, computers, or other electronic devices to people you have only met online.
- Remember that genuine trust is built through time and consistency, not through purchases.
- If someone becomes angry, blocks you, or disappears after you refuse a financial request, consider what that reaction reveals about their true intentions.
- Never feel obligated to spend money simply to keep a conversation alive.

Lesson Learned

A common manipulation technique is to present a problem and then guide you toward becoming the solution. The request may seem practical and reasonable, but the underlying goal is often financial rather than personal.

Final Thought: A genuine relationship grows through communication, honesty, and patience. If a connection suddenly depends on purchasing equipment or sending money, it may be worth asking whether the relationship is real—or whether the request was the goal from the beginning.

TENTH STORY: A VISITOR VISA TO YOUR COUNTRY

What makes this type of scam particularly effective is that it often appears after weeks or even months of communication.

The relationship seems to be progressing naturally. You exchange messages every day. You learn about each other's routines, families, goals, and dreams. Video calls may become frequent, and the conversations gradually shift from casual topics to discussions about the future.

One evening, she says something many people long to hear. "I wish we lived in the same country."

A few days later, the idea appears again. "It would be wonderful if we could finally meet in person."

Soon, conversations about the future become more serious. She talks about love, commitment, and the possibility of building a life together. She tells you that she wants to spend more time with you and believes the relationship has real potential.

For someone emotionally invested, these conversations can feel exciting and reassuring.

Then comes the obstacle. She explains that she cannot afford the visitor visa application, travel expenses, passport fees, or airline ticket. Sometimes she asks for help with only one expense. Other times, she presents a long list of costs that supposedly prevent the visit from happening.

The request is often framed as proof of commitment.

“If you really love me, you’ll help.”

“If we’re serious about each other, why wouldn’t we make this happen?”

At this stage, the discussion is no longer about travel. It becomes an emotional test designed to make you feel responsible for solving the problem.

If you hesitate, the pressure often increases. You may be accused of not trusting her. You may be told that you are not serious about the relationship. You may even be made to feel guilty for standing in the way of your supposed future together.

Unfortunately, many people discover too late that the promised trip never happens. Excuses appear, new expenses arise, deadlines are postponed, and additional payments are requested. In some cases, the person disappears entirely after receiving the money.

How Should You Respond?

- Never feel pressured to send money simply because someone claims it is necessary for a relationship to continue.
- Be cautious when discussions about love quickly become discussions about financial assistance.
- Remember that genuine affection should not depend on your willingness to pay for visas, travel costs, or other personal expenses.
- If someone repeatedly uses guilt, pressure, or emotional arguments to obtain money, consider it a serious warning sign.

- If you decide not to continue the relationship, politely but firmly refuse the request and end communication if the pressure continues.

Lesson Learned

One of the most powerful tools used by scammers is the promise of a shared future. They do not sell a visa, a plane ticket, or a travel expense—they sell hope. When emotions become tied to financial decisions, people often ignore warning signs they would otherwise recognize immediately.

Final Thought: A genuine relationship grows through trust, patience, and consistent actions. If the future someone promises always seems to require another payment first, it may be worth questioning whether the future was ever real at all.

ELEVENTH STORY: THE FAKE ACCOUNT

One evening, while browsing profiles on a dating site, I came across a profile that seemed almost perfect.

The photos were professional, the profile was well written, and everything appeared polished. Compared to many of the other profiles on the site, this one stood out immediately.

Naturally, I became curious.

Within a short time, a message arrived. "Hello. I noticed your profile and would love to get to know you."

At first, the conversation felt normal. The replies were friendly, and the person seemed interested in building a connection. Yet something felt slightly unusual.

The answers were often vague. Questions about daily life were avoided.

When I asked for details, the responses remained general and carefully worded.

As the conversation continued, I decided to take a closer look at the profile photo.

A reverse-image search revealed something surprising. The image did not belong to the person I had been speaking with.

In fact, it appeared on multiple websites and social media accounts under different names. In some cases, the photos used on fake dating profiles belong to models, influencers, or public figures whose images have been copied without permission.

Suddenly, the entire conversation looked different. The attractive profile that had seemed so genuine was little more than a carefully constructed disguise.

Unfortunately, this type of account is common across many dating platforms. The person operating the profile may not be the individual shown in the photos—and may not even be the gender they claim to be.

The objective varies from case to case. Some fake accounts are created to encourage users to purchase subscriptions. Others are used to build trust before requesting money, gifts, personal information, or financial assistance.

Whatever the goal, the deception begins with a false identity.

Many dating platforms actively warn users about suspicious behavior and encourage members to report questionable accounts. While these warnings are sometimes overlooked, they exist for a reason. Reporting suspicious activity helps protect both yourself and other users.

How Should You Respond?

- If a profile seems unusually perfect, take time to verify it before becoming emotionally invested.
- Use reverse-image search tools to check whether profile photos appear elsewhere on the internet.
- Be cautious of accounts that avoid personal questions or provide inconsistent information.
- Pay attention to profiles that quickly move conversations toward money, gifts, or financial assistance.

- Report suspicious accounts to the platform when appropriate.
- Never send money based solely on online conversations or profile photos.

Lesson Learned

A convincing profile is not proof of a genuine person. Photos can be copied, biographies can be invented, and identities can be fabricated. The more attractive and flawless a profile appears, the more important it becomes to verify what is real.

TWELFTH STORY: THE APP DEVELOPER TRAP (BEWARE!)

Not every scam on a dating site begins with a request for money. Some begin with curiosity.

A man matched with a woman who described herself as an independent mobile game developer. She seemed intelligent, ambitious, and passionate about her work.

Over the following weeks, she frequently talked about a project she had been working on.

According to her, she was preparing to launch her first mobile puzzle game. She shared screenshots, discussed design ideas, and spoke enthusiastically about the challenges of creating an app from scratch. Everything sounded believable.

One evening, she mentioned that she needed a few trusted people to test the application before its public release.

Naturally, he was interested.

After all, helping someone you care about with a personal project seems harmless.

She sent him a direct download link and explained that the application was not yet available through official app stores because it was still being tested. All he needed to do was install the file and try the game.

The request seemed innocent.

He downloaded the application. Nothing unusual happened at first.

The game appeared to work normally, and the conversation continued as if nothing had changed.

However, hidden behind the simple game was malicious software.

Without his knowledge, the application began collecting information from his phone. It monitored activity, captured passwords, and intercepted security codes sent by text message. The victim remained completely unaware that his device had effectively become an open door.

Several days later, he discovered unusual activity in his financial accounts.

By the time he realized what had happened, unauthorized transactions had already taken place, and significant amounts of money had disappeared.

The relationship that seemed genuine had been nothing more than a carefully constructed path toward gaining access to his device.

Unlike many scams that rely on emotional pressure or direct requests for money, this type of scheme exploits trust and curiosity. The victim is not asked to send funds. Instead, they unknowingly provide access to something far more valuable: their personal information.

How Should You Respond?

- Never install applications sent directly by strangers or people you have only met online.
- Be especially cautious when asked to download files from unofficial websites or direct links.

- Use official app stores whenever possible, as they provide additional security screening.
- Research any application before installing it, even if it appears to come from someone you trust.
- Keep your phone's operating system and security software updated.
- If you suspect that a device has been compromised, disconnect it from sensitive accounts and seek professional technical assistance immediately.

Lesson Learned

Modern scammers do not always ask for money directly. Sometimes they ask for access, trust, or curiosity instead. A single download can reveal more about your life than months of conversation.

Final Thought: Before installing anything sent by an online acquaintance, ask yourself a simple question: *Would I trust this file if it came from a complete stranger?* If the answer is no, do not let emotions change that answer.

THIRTEENTH STORY: THE MEDICAL EMERGENCY TRAP

The conversation began like many others. Soon she started discussing her health issues as a concern, and I listened and empathized with it.

Over the following days, health problems became a recurring topic. Every conversation seemed to include a new symptom, a doctor's appointment, or concerns about treatment.

Naturally, I felt sympathy. Most people would.

As trust developed, she shared more details. According to her, the treatment was expensive, she was unemployed, and there was no one available to help her financially. She described difficult decisions between paying for medication, food, and daily necessities.

The stories became increasingly emotional.

One day, she explained that her condition had suddenly worsened. Another day, she claimed she needed urgent tests.

"If I can't get treatment soon, things could become serious."

The request for money usually followed shortly afterward.

In some cases, the situation became even more dramatic.

A new person suddenly appeared in the conversation.

The individual introduced themselves as a friend, sister, cousin, or relative. They claimed the woman had been rushed to the hospital or admitted to an emergency room and urgently needed financial assistance.

The pressure intensified. The messages became more emotional. The timeline became more urgent.

The goal was simple: create a crisis so severe that logical thinking would be replaced by compassion and panic.

Whether the illness involved the woman herself, her mother, a child, or another family member, the strategy remained largely the same. A medical emergency was presented as the reason immediate financial assistance was required.

For many people, refusing such requests feels heartless.

Scammers understand this. That is precisely why health-related stories are among the most effective emotional manipulation tactics used online.

How Should You Respond?

- Be cautious when conversations quickly become focused on medical problems and financial hardship.
- Remember that emotional stories, no matter how convincing, do not automatically verify the facts.
- Avoid sending money based solely on messages, photos, or claims of urgent medical emergencies.
- Be especially careful if new people suddenly join the conversation, claiming to be relatives, friends, or hospital contacts.
- If repeated requests for financial assistance appear, consider ending the conversation.

- Trust should be built through time, consistency, and verification—not through emotional pressure.

Lesson Learned

Medical emergencies create powerful emotional reactions. Most people naturally want to help someone who appears to be suffering. Unfortunately, scammers understand this and sometimes use illness, hospitalization, and family tragedies to bypass caution and encourage immediate financial decisions.

Final Thought: Compassion is a valuable quality, but compassion should not replace critical thinking. When someone you've only met online asks for money to solve a medical crisis, remember that emotions can be genuine—even when the story behind them is not.

FOURTEENTH STORY: A FRIENDSHIP OF CONVENIENCE

Not everyone on a dating site claims to be looking for love.

Some profiles clearly state that the person is only seeking friendship, companionship, or someone to talk to. At first, this can seem refreshing. There are no grand promises, no declarations of affection, and no immediate discussions about relationships.

One such conversation began this way.

She described herself as a single mother looking for friendship and meaningful conversation. We exchanged messages about our daily lives, interests, and experiences. The conversations were pleasant and free from the usual romantic pressure found on many dating platforms.

As trust developed, she began sharing more personal details. She talked about her children. She spoke about the challenges of raising them alone after their father had left the family. She described financial struggles, school expenses, and the difficulties of providing everything her children needed.

Naturally, the stories were emotional. Most parents understand the desire to protect and provide for their children, making such conversations particularly difficult to ignore.

Over time, the messages became more personal. She explained that she appreciated my kindness and felt comfortable talking to me. Eventually, she hinted that she would be open to a closer relationship. She even suggested that, under the right circumstances, she might consider a future together.

There was only one condition. Anyone who became part of her life would also need to accept her children.

For many people, that is a reasonable expectation.

The problem arose when the conversation shifted from discussing family responsibilities to requesting financial assistance.

Suddenly, there were urgent needs. School supplies. Food expenses. Utility bills. Unexpected costs involving the children.

The message was subtle but clear: Helping financially would demonstrate sincerity, commitment, and compassion.

What started as friendship gradually became a test of generosity.

The emotional stories remained focused on the children because few people want to appear indifferent to a child in need. Unfortunately, some individuals understand this and use family hardships to encourage financial support from people they have only met online.

This does not mean every single parent on a dating site is dishonest. Many are genuine people looking for meaningful relationships. The warning sign appears when emotional stories repeatedly lead to requests for money.

How Should You Respond?

- Never reveal detailed financial information to someone you have only met online.

- Be cautious when conversations repeatedly focus on financial hardship.
- Avoid sending money to people you have not met and verified in real life.
- Remember that sympathy and trust should not automatically lead to financial responsibility.
- Pay attention to whether the relationship seems focused on getting to know you or on obtaining assistance.
- If financial requests become a recurring theme, consider ending the conversation.

Lesson Learned

One of the most effective forms of manipulation is to make someone feel responsible for solving another person's problems. When children are involved, emotions become even stronger, making it easier to overlook warning signs.

FIFTEENTH STORY: THE SUDDEN DISAPPEARANCE

Everything seemed to be going perfectly.

After meeting on a dating site, we began exchanging messages regularly. The conversations were enjoyable, and with each passing day, I felt more comfortable talking to her. She seemed genuine, attentive, and interested in building a connection.

Days turned into weeks.

We shared stories about our lives, discussed future plans, and developed a routine. Before long, checking for her messages became part of my day.

Then, without warning, she disappeared. No messages. No explanation. No response.

At first, I assumed she was simply busy. But as the days passed, concern began to replace patience. I wondered whether something had happened to her. Had she become ill? Was there a family emergency? Had she lost interest?

The uncertainty was difficult to ignore.

Just as my worry reached its peak, a message finally appeared.

She apologized for disappearing and explained that she had been unable to contact me. According to her story, her phone had been accidentally dropped, damaged beyond repair, or ruined by water. In some versions, a child had broken it. In others, it had simply stopped working without warning.

Now, she claimed, she was borrowing someone else's device to send a few messages.

The explanation seemed believable. After all, unexpected accidents happen every day.

She expressed sadness about losing contact and reassured me that she still wanted to continue getting to know me. She talked about how much she had missed our conversations and how frustrating the situation had been.

Then came the solution. If she had a new phone, she explained, everything could return to normal. We could talk freely again. We could continue building our connection. All she needed was a little help.

The request was usually framed as a temporary problem with a simple answer: send money so she could replace the device.

For someone emotionally invested in the relationship, the timing felt significant. The relief of hearing from her again often overshadowed the warning signs.

How Should You Respond?

• Be cautious when a long period of unexplained silence is followed by a request for money.

- Remember that emotional attachment can make financial requests seem more reasonable than they actually are.
- Avoid sending money for phones, computers, repairs, or replacement devices to people you have only met online.

- Pay attention to whether similar emergencies seem to occur repeatedly.
- Do not allow feelings of concern or guilt to pressure you into making financial decisions.
- If the conversation repeatedly returns to money, consider ending communication.

Lesson Learned

One of the most effective manipulation techniques is creating uncertainty. When someone disappears after earning your trust, concern naturally grows. The relief you feel when they return can make you more vulnerable to requests you might otherwise question.

SIXTEENTH STORY: EXPLOITING CIRCUMSTANCES AND NATURAL DISASTERS

The conversation usually begins in a completely normal way. You exchange greetings, ask a few basic questions, and slowly begin to get to know each other. Everything feels ordinary at first, with no indication that anything unusual is about to happen.

Then, gradually, the tone changes. She mentions where she lives and explains that her region has recently been affected by a natural disaster—an earthquake, flood, or severe storm. The details often feel vivid and specific. She may describe tremors shaking her home, water rising into streets, or mud still covering her doorway. In some cases, she may refer to power outages, damaged infrastructure, or days without electricity.

At first, these details seem entirely believable. After all, natural disasters happen around the world, and it is easy to verify such events with a quick online search. In many cases, you may indeed find news confirming that something happened in that area, which makes the story feel even more credible.

As the conversation continues, the situation becomes more personal.

She explains that she has lost her job due to the crisis. Her workplace has closed, leaving her without income. She may say she is struggling to pay rent, buy food, or cover basic daily needs. Often, she adds that she lives alone or is responsible for children, increasing the emotional weight of the situation.

The story becomes less about the disaster itself and more about survival.

Naturally, sympathy begins to build. That is precisely the intention. At this stage, the conversation may shift from sharing experiences to requesting help. The request is usually framed as urgent and necessary, tied directly to the hardship caused by the disaster. It may appear small compared to the scale of the crisis being described, which makes it feel reasonable to consider.

However, in many cases, the emotional narrative is carefully constructed to create trust and urgency at the same time.

Even when the disaster itself is real, the individual circumstances may not be verifiable. The connection between the person and the situation may be exaggerated, incomplete, or entirely fabricated.

This combination of truth and uncertainty is what makes this type of manipulation particularly effective.

How Should You Respond?

- Be cautious when conversations begin to focus heavily on disasters, crises, or emergencies.
- Remember that real-world events can be used to support false personal stories.
- Avoid sending money based solely on emotional narratives, no matter how realistic they appear.
- Look for consistency in the story over time, not just emotional detail in the moment.
- Be especially careful when requests for financial assistance appear shortly after sympathy is established.

- If the conversation repeatedly centers on hardship and money, consider stepping away.

Lesson Learned

One of the most persuasive forms of manipulation combines truth with emotion. A real disaster can make a false personal story feel authentic, and emotional detail can make financial requests feel justified. This overlap is what often leads people to lower their guard.

Final Thought: Compassion should never replace verification. Even when a situation sounds real and emotionally compelling, it is important to separate verified facts from personal claims before making any financial decision.

SEVENTEENTH STORY: LOOKING FOR A JOB

At first glance, everything appears normal.

You are browsing profiles on a dating site, reading introductions, and getting a sense of different people. Among them, you notice some profiles that mention an interest in work opportunities or a desire to build a better future abroad.

In the beginning, this may not seem unusual. Many people around the world are genuinely looking for stability and better opportunities.

As the conversation begins, things feel friendly and casual. You exchange basic information, talk about daily life, and gradually learn more about each other.

Then, at some point, the topic shifts.

She begins to talk about her financial situation. She explains that jobs are difficult to find in her country, wages are low, and opportunities are limited. The conversation slowly turns toward the idea of working abroad.

Eventually, she asks for help.

The request is usually not direct at first. Instead, it may appear as a question: "Do you know any job openings in your country?"

"Can you help me find work there?"

Over time, the expectation becomes clearer. The conversation moves from general curiosity to a request for sponsorship, assistance, or support in finding employment abroad.

For some, the implication becomes even stronger: that a meaningful connection could develop if only this obstacle could be solved.

At this stage, emotional pressure can begin to appear. If assistance is not offered, the conversation may become less responsive or stop entirely. This can make the situation feel like a test of interest or commitment.

How Should You Respond?

- Be cautious when conversations quickly shift toward employment or immigration topics.
- Avoid sharing job-related assistance or financial support with someone you have only met online.
- Be careful when interest in the relationship appears dependent on your ability to provide opportunities.
- Do not feel pressured to "prove" interest through help, money, or sponsorship.
- If the conversation feels conditional or transactional, consider stepping back.
- It is acceptable to politely disengage if the dynamic feels uncomfortable or one-sided.

Lesson Learned

A genuine connection is not dependent on providing solutions to someone's financial or professional challenges. While many people are sincerely seeking better opportunities, others may use this as a pathway toward dependency or emotional leverage.

Final Thought: Interest in a relationship should not disappear simply because help is not offered. When connection depends on what you can provide rather than who you are, it is worth reconsidering the intention behind the conversation.

EIGHTEENTH STORY: DIGITAL CURRENCIES

After establishing contact on a dating site and spending some time getting to know each other, the conversation may begin to shift in a familiar direction.

She starts sharing personal difficulties.

Financial struggles. Unexpected life problems. Emotional situations designed to gain sympathy.

As the conversation develops, the tone gradually becomes more serious. Requests for help begin to appear, often framed as urgent or unavoidable circumstances.

This pattern is not new. However, in some cases, the method of requesting assistance changes. Instead of asking for money through traditional bank transfers or payment services, the request may involve digital currencies such as Ethereum or Dogecoin.

Because of this, the request may feel different from earlier scenarios. It may even appear more secure or traceable in comparison, especially for those unfamiliar with how these systems work.

However, the underlying pattern remains the same. The conversation is still centered on emotional storytelling followed by a financial request.

The method of payment does not change the nature of the request itself.

In many cases, individuals may feel additional pressure because cryptocurrency transactions are less familiar, harder to reverse, and not always fully understood by beginners. This can create confusion or hesitation, making the situation more difficult to evaluate calmly.

The key issue is not the technology being used, but the expectation behind it: that emotional connection should lead to financial contribution.

How Should You Respond?

- Be cautious when conversations shift from personal connection to financial requests of any kind.
- Remember that digital currency requests are still financial requests, even if they appear more modern or technical.
- Do not feel pressured to send money through unfamiliar systems.
- Avoid making financial decisions under emotional stress or urgency.
- If repeated requests occur, consider ending the conversation entirely.
- Protect your personal information and avoid learning payment systems solely for someone you have not met in real life.

Lesson Learned

The tools may change, but the pattern often remains the same. Whether through traditional transfers or digital currencies, the goal is often to convert emotional engagement into financial support.

Final Thought: Technology does not reduce risk—it only changes its form. A request for cryptocurrency is still a request for money, and emotional pressure does not make it any less significant.

NINETEENTH STORY: SUSPICIOUS EMAILS

Although email-based scams have been mentioned earlier in this booklet, it is important to examine them in more detail, as they often appear convincing and can take many different forms.

Unlike dating-site messages, these emails can come from unknown senders, fake identities, or even impersonated accounts. In some cases, they may include a personal photo or claim to represent someone familiar, which is intended to create trust and curiosity.

Common examples include:

- An email claiming you have already met the sender before, often referencing mutual friends or shared experiences, along with links to "photos" of that encounter.

- A message that appears to come from someone inviting you to visit them, including an address and travel details.
- A long, overly detailed email filled with unnecessary or repetitive information, designed to appear authentic but ultimately raising suspicion due to its unnatural tone.
- A message claiming the sender previously contacted you, apologizing for a delayed response, and explaining it was due to spam filters, lack of internet access, or technical issues.

At first glance, these messages may seem harmless or even familiar. However, a closer look often reveals inconsistencies.

When you attempt to reply, the responses are frequently vague, indirect, or unrelated to your questions. Instead of clear communication, you may receive generic messages designed to keep the conversation going without addressing anything specific.

In many cases, the real purpose of these emails is not conversation but engagement—encouraging you to click links, open attachments, or share personal information.

These actions can expose users to serious risks, including malware, phishing attempts, identity theft, or unauthorized access to personal accounts.

How Should You Respond?

- Do not click on links or open attachments from unknown or suspicious emails.
- Avoid engaging in conversations with messages that feel inconsistent or unnatural.
- Be cautious of emails that rely heavily on emotional storytelling or overly detailed explanations.
- Treat unexpected claims of prior connection with skepticism, especially when no context is provided.
- Mark suspicious emails as spam or report them through your email provider.
- When in doubt, do not respond—silence is often the safest option.

Lesson Learned

Email scams often rely on familiarity, urgency, or curiosity to bypass judgment. Even when a message appears personal or emotionally engaging, it is important to verify its authenticity before taking any action.

Not every message is meant to be answered. Sometimes, the safest response is no response at all.

TWENTIETH STORY: ON BEHALF OF HER SISTER

A girl contacts you through a dating site, introducing herself as the person in the profile photo. The exchange starts normally, with basic questions, polite responses, and the usual effort to get to know each other.

Then, the conversation takes an unexpected turn. She mentions her sister. According to her, her sister has seen your profile and is also interested in you. She explains that her sister liked your picture, your personality, or something you wrote in your bio. Soon after, she begins acting as a kind of intermediary between you and her sister.

At this stage, the communication becomes slightly unusual but still appears harmless.

She may ask for additional personal details, social media accounts, or contact information, claiming that she is simply helping her sister find a suitable partner. In some cases, she may even suggest that her sister is too shy to speak directly, so she is assisting in the conversation.

Gradually, however, inconsistencies begin to appear.

The identity of the "sister" is never clearly established.

Questions are often avoided or redirected. Details remain vague, and the conversation feels less like two individuals communicating and more like a controlled interaction designed to extract information.

In some situations, the goal may be to gather personal data, build trust under false pretenses, or shift the conversation toward more private platforms where further manipulation becomes easier.

What makes this approach effective is the illusion of legitimacy. The presence of a "third person" creates a sense of social validation, making the interaction feel more real and less suspicious.

However, without proper verification, there is no way to confirm whether the sister exists at all.

How Should You Respond?

- Be cautious when third parties are introduced into online conversations without clear verification.
- Avoid sharing personal information or social media accounts with people you have only met online.
- Ask direct and consistent questions to verify identities when something feels unclear.
- Pay attention to vague explanations, shifting details, or avoidance of simple questions.
- If the story feels inconsistent or overly complicated, consider discontinuing the conversation.
- Prioritize privacy and do not feel obligated to continue interactions that make you uncomfortable.

Lesson Learned

A common manipulation tactic is to introduce additional characters into a conversation to create trust or legitimacy. However, without verification, these claims can easily be fabricated.

In genuine communication, identities are clear and consistent. When people or stories cannot be verified, caution is always the safest response.

TWENTY-FIRST STORY: CLOSING THE DATING SITE ACCOUNT

At first, everything appears to be moving in a positive direction.

You begin talking to someone on a dating site, and the conversation develops naturally. Messages are exchanged regularly, and a sense of familiarity slowly begins to form. The interaction feels consistent, and there is nothing unusual in the early stages.

Then, unexpectedly, she mentions that she is going to close her account.

Sometimes the decision is immediate. Other times, it is framed as something already in progress. The explanation is often simple: She prefers to continue the conversation elsewhere, or she feels more comfortable focusing on one person rather than remaining active on the platform.

In many cases, she adds a reassuring statement such as: "I like you, and I want to know you more."

At this point, the shift feels personal and exclusive, as if the connection has become something special.

However, the situation may take an unexpected turn later.

While browsing the same dating platform again, you notice a profile that looks familiar. The photo appears almost identical to the person you were speaking with, but the details are different.

The name has changed. The age is different. The location no longer matches.

At first, it may seem like a coincidence. But when you compare the image more carefully—perhaps with photos previously shared or even images from social media—you begin to recognize the same person behind the profile.

The conclusion becomes difficult to ignore: It is the same individual using multiple identities.

This discovery raises important questions. If someone claims to be closing their account to focus on you, why does another profile appear under a different identity? If the connection was exclusive, why is the same person still actively present on the platform in a different form?

In many cases, this behavior suggests inconsistency, misrepresentation, or the management of multiple simultaneous conversations under different identities. Sometimes, it may also indicate testing behavior or attempts to maintain multiple options without transparency.

Regardless of the reason, the core issue remains the same: Trust becomes uncertain when identity is not consistent.

How Should You Respond?

- Do not ignore clear inconsistencies in identity or profile information.
- If possible, verify profile photos and details using available online tools or cross-checking methods.
- Be cautious when someone claims exclusivity but continues to appear on the platform under different profiles.

- Avoid emotional decisions based solely on statements of attachment or exclusivity.
- If trust is broken due to inconsistency, it is reasonable to step away from the conversation.
- Protect your emotional and personal boundaries when honesty is in doubt.

Lesson Learned

Consistency is one of the strongest indicators of honesty in online communication. When identity, behavior, or intentions appear to change depending on the situation, it becomes difficult to establish genuine trust.

A real connection does not require multiple identities. When one person appears in many forms, it is worth questioning which version—if any—is real.

TWENTY-SECOND STORY: "YOU WILL BECOME RICH!"

This may be one of the most extreme and deceptive stories in this entire collection.

While browsing a dating site, you may suddenly receive a message from someone claiming to be very interested in your profile. The message is usually direct and unusually eager, often pushing for quick communication outside the platform.

Soon after, she may ask for your email address, sometimes even sending hers first to create a sense of trust and urgency. The tone of the conversation can feel unusually friendly, almost as if the relationship has already been established.

Once contact is moved to email, the interaction becomes more structured.

She may thank you for responding and request a few personal photos and basic details about yourself. In return, she may promise to share her own photos or personal information, reinforcing the idea of mutual trust.

At this stage, everything still appears ordinary. However, the tone of the messages soon changes. You receive a long email containing a highly emotional and dramatic story. In many cases, it involves the sudden death of a wealthy family member—often a father or close relative—who has allegedly left behind a large inheritance.

According to the message, the funds are stored in another country or locked in a financial system that requires assistance to access or transfer.

She then presents a proposal. She claims she needs your help to move the money into her personal account and promises that, in return, you will receive a percentage of the funds as a reward. The message often emphasizes secrecy, urgency, and trust. You may also be told that she plans to visit you once everything is resolved.

The emotional appeal is carefully constructed. The promise of wealth, combined with a sense of exclusivity and urgency, is designed to bypass logical thinking and encourage immediate cooperation.

However, this type of message is a well-known form of financial fraud. The story is entirely fabricated, and the promised money does not exist.

How Should You Respond?

- Do not respond to unsolicited emails involving inheritance, large sums of money, or financial transfers.
- Never share personal documents, banking details, or identification information with unknown contacts.
- Avoid engaging in conversations that involve secrecy, urgency, or financial rewards.
- Do not click on attachments or links contained in suspicious emails.
- Report and delete such messages immediately.

- Remember that legitimate financial institutions and legal processes do not operate through random online contacts.

Lesson Learned

This type of scam relies on hope and imagination rather than reality. The promise of sudden wealth is used to create excitement and override caution.

TWENTY-THIRD STORY: DEVOTED TO YOU ALONE

At first, the conversation feels like any other. You meet someone on a dating site, exchange a few messages, and begin getting to know each other gradually. The tone is friendly, and the interaction appears normal. There is no immediate pressure, and nothing initially suggests anything unusual.

However, as the conversation continues, the direction begins to change.

She starts asking more personal and relationship-focused questions. Instead of casual topics, the discussion moves quickly toward commitment and long-term intentions.

"Are you serious about marrying me?"

"Would you be willing to move to my country?"

"Are you ready to meet my family and begin wedding preparations?"

These questions appear early and intensify quickly, creating a sense of urgency around commitment.

Shortly afterward, she introduces another idea. She explains that she is planning to close her dating account because she only wants to focus on one person. According to her, she prefers exclusivity and does not want to continue speaking with multiple people.

On the surface, this may sound sincere or even flattering.

Then comes the condition. She says she will close her account only if you prove your seriousness. That proof, she explains, is a small financial contribution.

It may be framed as a symbolic gesture, a sign of commitment, or reassurance that you are genuinely serious about the relationship. She may also emphasize that once this is done, she will dedicate all her time to you, stop speaking to others, and focus entirely on building a future together.

The conversation is carefully structured to create emotional pressure.

Exclusivity is offered. Commitment is expected. And money is introduced as the deciding factor. This combination is what makes the situation manipulative.

In genuine relationships, emotional connection is not conditioned on financial proof. Trust is built through time, consistency, and real-life interaction—not payments or symbolic transactions.

How Should You Respond?

- Be cautious when exclusivity or commitment is linked to financial requests.
- Do not treat money as proof of sincerity or emotional interest.
- Avoid situations where access to someone's attention depends on payment.
- Recognize that genuine relationships do not require financial validation.
- If someone pressures you to "prove" love through money, step away from the conversation.

- Protect yourself from emotional decisions made under urgency or pressure.

Lesson Learned

Healthy relationships grow through mutual understanding and shared experiences, not financial conditions. When money becomes a requirement for attention or exclusivity, the dynamic is no longer balanced or authentic.

Final Thought: Real connection is given freely. If it must be purchased, it is not connection—it is negotiation.

TWENTY-FOURTH STORY: WORKING IN THE ARMY

You meet someone on a dating site who introduces herself as serving in the army. She explains that she is often busy due to duty, sometimes stationed in different locations, and occasionally involved in special assignments.

The conversation begins in a normal and friendly way. She shares personal experiences, talks about her past, and often mentions emotional difficulties she has faced in relationships. According to her, she has been betrayed before and is now looking for something serious—built on trust, loyalty, and respect.

As the interaction continues, the tone becomes warmer. She sends personal photos, communicates frequently when possible, and gradually builds a sense of emotional closeness. To the reader, it may begin to feel like a genuine and meaningful connection.

However, over time, the situation starts to shift. Requests begin to appear. They are usually framed as small, reasonable favors: “Can you send me a gift card? I can’t purchase one from here.”

“Can you help me buy medicine? I send my salary to my father or child.”

These requests may seem harmless at first, especially when placed in a context of duty, distance, or limited access to resources. The story is often designed to make the situation appear restricted or urgent.

But when examined carefully, inconsistencies may arise.

Military institutions typically provide structured support systems for personnel, including access to essential supplies and financial resources. Situations that repeatedly rely on external financial assistance from someone met online should therefore be viewed with caution.

What makes this type of scenario effective is the combination of authority and vulnerability. The idea of someone serving in uniform creates trust, while emotional storytelling creates sympathy.

Together, they can lower natural caution.

How Should You Respond?

- Be cautious when professional identities are used to justify financial requests.
- Do not send money, gift cards, or financial assistance to someone you have not met in real life.
- Use reverse-image search tools to verify whether photos appear elsewhere online.
- Pay attention to repeated patterns of emotional storytelling followed by financial requests.
- Remember that legitimate institutions do not require personal financial support from strangers met online.
- If requests for money begin, consider ending the conversation.

Lesson Learned

Authority and emotion can be combined to create a powerful illusion of trust. However, genuine relationships are not built on financial dependency or repeated requests for help.

Final Thought: A real connection does not require you to fund someone's life from a distance. When money enters the relationship too early, clarity should replace emotion.

TWENTY-FIFTH STORY: THE INHERITANCE

A girl begins chatting with you on a dating site and starts asking practical, personal questions early on.

"Do you have a job?"

"What is your salary?"

Although these questions may seem casual, they are often used to gauge financial capacity and lifestyle.

As the conversation continues, she introduces a remarkable story.

According to her, she has received a large inheritance from her father—sometimes biological, sometimes adoptive. The details vary, but the theme is consistent: valuable assets such as properties in another country, business holdings, or even a gold mine in Africa.

She explains that she is currently abroad handling legal procedures with a lawyer to prove ownership and complete the required formalities.

Over the next few days, she remains in regular contact.

Everything appears to be progressing smoothly. She updates you about meetings, legal steps, and documentation. The story builds credibility through consistency and detail, creating the impression that something real is unfolding.

Then comes the turning point.

She suddenly shares exciting news: The process has been completed. To support her claim, she may even send a photograph of an official-looking ownership document.

At this stage, everything is designed to appear legitimate.

But shortly afterward, a complication arises. She explains that she has exhausted her funds due to travel, accommodation, or legal expenses. According to her, the lawyer now requires a small remaining payment to finalize and release the documents.

She then asks you to help by sending that amount. This is the final step in the narrative.

A large inheritance is already established. The finish line seems close. Only a small financial obstacle remains.

This structure is what makes the scenario persuasive.

However, in most cases, the documents are fabricated or taken from unrelated sources, and the entire inheritance story is designed to create urgency and trust simultaneously.

How Should You Respond?

- Use reverse-image search tools to verify any documents or photos provided.
- Be cautious of stories involving sudden wealth that require small payments to unlock large sums.
- Remember that legitimate inheritance processes do not involve financial requests from strangers.
- Do not send money under emotional pressure or urgency.
- End communication if financial requests appear after prolonged storytelling.

- Treat claims of overseas legal procedures with skepticism unless independently verified.

Lesson Learned

This type of manipulation combines hope with authority. The idea of a large inheritance creates excitement, while legal details create a sense of legitimacy. Together, they are used to lower critical thinking.

Real wealth does not depend on assistance from strangers. When a fortune requires your money to be released, it is not a blessing—it is a warning.

TWENTY-SIXTH STORY: BUYING AN ELECTRONIC DEVICE

For several weeks, the conversation followed a steady rhythm.

Every day, at nearly the same time, she would appear online. The discussions felt natural at first—talking about work, family, hobbies, and everyday life. Over time, a sense of routine developed, and the conversations became something to look forward to.

Then one day, she ended the chat abruptly. “I’m sorry, I have to go. I’m using an internet café, and my time is running out.”

The explanation seemed harmless, even believable.

The next day, she returned and repeated a similar pattern. She explained that accessing the internet from the café was becoming difficult. It was expensive, inconvenient, and far from her home.

This topic slowly became a regular part of the conversation.

Each time, the same issue resurfaced: limited access, restricted time, and difficulty staying connected.

Then a solution was introduced. "If I had my own device, we could talk anytime."

At first, it was mentioned casually. Later, it became more direct. The idea expanded from a simple smartphone to more expensive devices like a tablet, laptop, or personal computer—something that would supposedly solve all communication problems and make the relationship easier and more stable.

Around the same period, her behavior also changed.

She began disappearing for longer intervals—sometimes days—returning with explanations such as family issues, internet problems, or unexpected difficulties. Each return made the conversation feel more emotionally significant, as if the connection were being strengthened through absence.

Looking closely, a clear pattern emerges. A limitation is introduced. The limitation is repeated over time. And eventually, a financial solution is suggested.

In some cases, inconsistencies may also appear. Someone claiming to have limited internet access may still be active at unusual hours or remain present on the platform despite describing severe communication barriers.

When behavior and explanation do not align, caution is necessary.

How Should You Respond?

- Be cautious when communication repeatedly revolves around problems that require financial solutions.
- Pay attention to whether online activity matches what is being claimed.
- Observe patterns of disappearance followed by emotionally intense returns.
- Avoid buying phones, laptops, tablets, or any electronic devices for someone you have only met online.

- Do not let emotional attachment replace rational judgment.
- If inconsistencies continue, consider ending the conversation.

Lesson Learned

Many manipulative conversations do not begin with money—they begin with a problem. Once emotional attachment forms, solutions are introduced that require financial involvement.

Final Thought: A genuine connection does not depend on solving someone's material limitations. When the relationship repeatedly turns into a request for devices or financial help, it is worth questioning where the connection is truly heading.

TWENTY-SEVENTH STORY: THE HIGH-END RESTAURANT SETUP (THE "DROP-OFF" SCAM)

It started like any other promising match.

A man in a busy Asian metropolis connected with an attractive woman on a local dating app. Her profile felt polished, confident, and selective. She responded quickly, but always with one condition: She preferred to choose the place for their first meeting.

"I know a very nice lounge," she said. "It's quiet, private, and perfect for a first date."

The confidence in her tone made it feel like a thoughtful suggestion rather than a demand.

He agreed.

On the evening of the date, they met at an upscale lounge tucked inside a luxury district. The atmosphere was dim, elegant, and expensive. Soft music played in the background, and the staff greeted her like a regular guest.

That detail, at the time, felt reassuring.

Once seated, she immediately took control of the order. She recommended premium champagne, imported dishes, and eventually added items like caviar and high-end appetizers "just to try." The man hesitated briefly, but the staff responded quickly and professionally, reinforcing the sense that this was normal for the venue.

The conversation flowed. She was charming, attentive, and engaged. Everything felt like a successful first meeting.

Then, midway through the evening, she excused herself.

"I'll be back in a minute," she said, heading toward the restroom.

Minutes passed. Then more. She never returned.

At first, he assumed she had received a call or stepped out briefly. But after waiting, he asked the staff if she was still inside. Their response shifted the tone of the entire evening.

They informed him that the woman was known to the establishment—but not as a guest.

She was allegedly part of a setup designed to bring in customers from dating apps, encourage high-value orders, and then disappear before the bill arrived.

The realization came too late.

With no date returning and a table filled with expensive items already consumed, the responsibility fell entirely on him. Security ensured the bill was settled before he could leave.

The total exceeded $1,500 for a single hour. What began as a casual first meeting ended as a carefully staged financial trap.

How Should You Respond?

- Be cautious when a stranger insists on selecting an expensive or unfamiliar venue for a first meeting.
- Prefer meeting in publicly known, reasonably priced locations that you choose or mutually agree upon.

- Be alert when rapid ordering of high-cost items begins early in the interaction.
- Avoid accepting financial pressure in social settings where you have limited control over arrangements.
- If something feels unusually structured or scripted, step back and reassess the situation.

Lesson Learned

Not all dating scams happen online—some are designed to complete themselves in person. The environment, the choices, and even the timing can be part of a carefully constructed setup.

Final Thought: A genuine first meeting should feel comfortable and balanced, not like a performance where the ending has already been written by someone else.

TWENTY-EIGHTH STORY: THE FAKE VERIFICATION WEBSITE (THE "SAFE DATING" TRAP)

It began like a normal conversation on a major dating app.

A man matched with a woman who seemed friendly, cautious, and slightly reserved. Their messages were brief at first, but they quickly moved toward arranging a simple first meeting at a local coffee shop.

Before confirming, however, she brought up a concern.

She explained that she had been hurt in the past after meeting someone online and was now careful about her safety. Because of that experience, she said she only met people who could first "verify" themselves.

Then she sent a link.

According to her, it was a "Free Dating Protection Pass"—a system designed to confirm that users were not criminals or fake profiles. She encouraged him to complete it before they met, framing it as a normal safety step.

The website looked convincing. It had clean design, professional branding, and familiar-looking security icons. There were fake trust badges, reassuring statements, and even a progress bar showing "verification in process." Everything was carefully designed to create a sense of legitimacy.

The form requested basic personal details: name, email, and address.

Then came the final step. A small verification charge—just a few dollars on a credit card—to confirm identity and activate the pass.

It seemed harmless. A routine step before meeting someone in person.

But the moment he entered his payment details, the purpose of the site changed completely.

Instead of a simple verification, the system silently processed his card information. What appeared to be a one-time fee was actually a gateway into hidden subscriptions and unauthorized charges.

Within days, additional transactions began appearing. Small at first. Then larger.

Eventually, multiple recurring international charges were linked to services he had never knowingly signed up for, accumulating into hundreds of dollars per month.

The woman who sent the link, meanwhile, became unreachable. The conversation stopped. The profile disappeared.

And the "verification requirement" was revealed for what it truly was: a carefully designed phishing trap disguised as safety.

How Should You Respond?

- Never trust external "verification" websites sent by people you have just met online.
- Avoid entering personal or payment information outside official platforms.

- Be cautious of urgency or emotional framing around safety requirements.
- Remember that legitimate dating platforms do not require third-party paid verification to meet someone.
- Do not click or register on links shared by strangers, even if they appear professional.
- If payment details have been entered, contact your bank immediately and monitor for unauthorized charges.

Lesson Learned

This type of scam uses trust and fear at the same time—trust in authority and fear of appearing unsafe or suspicious. Together, they pressure individuals into lowering their guard.

TWENTY-NINTH STORY: THE "MANGLED SHIPPING" (CUSTOMS FEE SCAM)

It began with an unexpected kind of generosity.

A man on a dating app matched with a woman who introduced herself as a luxury-goods dealer traveling through Asia. Her profile was polished, international, and filled with references to high-end brands and global business trips. She spoke confidently about her work, often mentioning exclusive items and international clients.

After a few days of conversation, the tone shifted. She became warmer, more personal, and increasingly affectionate. Then she surprised him with a gesture that felt both romantic and extravagant.

She said she wanted to send him a gift. A designer watch and a high-end laptop, both expensive items from premium brands, supposedly shipped directly from her current location, as a token of appreciation.

It felt unusual, but not impossible. After all, she presented herself as someone who regularly handled luxury goods.

A few days later, he received an email. It appeared to come from an international courier service. The branding looked official, complete with tracking numbers, shipment updates, and a detailed delivery timeline. The message stated that a package addressed to him had been intercepted at Customs.

According to the notice, the declared value of the items had raised regulatory concerns. "Undeclared luxury value detected."

The email explained that the shipment could not proceed unless a customs clearance fee was paid. The amount was significant—$2,500—but it was framed as a mandatory legal requirement. The message also warned that failure to comply could result in penalties or legal consequences related to illegal import activity.

The pressure was immediate and structured.

A tracking link showed the package in transit. Official-looking documents supported the claim.

And the idea of receiving expensive gifts made the situation emotionally compelling.

Wanting to resolve the issue quickly—and avoid any potential legal trouble—he paid the fee. After the payment was made, everything changed.

The tracking system stopped updating. The courier website disappeared or became inaccessible. The woman who had sent the gift request stopped responding entirely.

The promised luxury items never existed.

What remained was only the realization that both the romantic connection and the "shipping issue" had been carefully constructed parts of the same deception.

How Should You Respond?

- Be highly cautious of unexpected luxury gifts that require payment for release.
- Never pay Customs, clearance, or legal fees for items you did not personally purchase.

- Verify courier emails directly through official company websites, not through provided links.
- Avoid emotional decisions when financial pressure is linked to urgency or legal threats.
- Remember that legitimate Customs processes do not require random individuals to pay fees for unsolicited shipments.
- When in doubt, contact the official courier service independently using verified contact details.

Lesson Learned

This type of scam blends romance with authority. A generous gift creates excitement, while official-looking documents create fear. Together, they pressure the victim into paying for something that never existed.

THIRTIETH STORY: THE FAKE FLIGHT TICKET ROUTINE (CANADA)

It started with what felt like a genuine long-distance connection.

A young professional matched with a woman on a dating site who claimed to live a few provinces away in Canada. The distance was real but manageable. Over several weeks, their conversations became consistent, warm, and increasingly personal. They talked about daily life, future plans, and eventually the idea of meeting in person.

After enough time, the plan finally took shape. She said she would fly out to visit him.

The idea felt like a natural next step—something to turn an online connection into something real.

They chose a date, discussed timing, and prepared for the visit. Everything seemed organized and sincere.

Then, on the day of travel, something changed.

She messaged him from the airport.

According to her, her credit card had been declined at the last moment, and she could not complete the ticket payment. She sounded distressed and embarrassed, explaining that she needed help immediately or she would miss the flight.

Wanting to avoid ruining the visit, he sent her the requested amount—around $600—for the ticket.

The situation escalated the next day. She contacted him again, this time with a more serious issue. She claimed that upon arrival, she had been stopped by Customs, due to an unresolved financial fine. She said she was being detained and could not proceed unless the fee was paid immediately.

The amount had increased. Now it was another $1,000.

The urgency was higher, the tone more alarming, and the pressure significantly stronger. The emotional weight of the situation made it feel like helping was the only way to resolve it.

He sent the money again.

After that, everything went silent. Her messages stopped. Her profile disappeared from the dating site. No flight details could be verified, no arrival ever happened, and no further contact was possible.

What had begun as a promising real-world meeting turned out to be a carefully staged sequence designed to extract money through escalating emergencies.

How Should You Respond?

- Be cautious when online relationships quickly move toward urgent financial travel problems.
- Never send money for tickets, airport fees, or travel emergencies to someone you have not met in person.
- Verify flight bookings directly through official airline websites whenever possible.
- Be especially careful when one financial request is followed immediately by another.

- Treat airport "detention" or Customs fines claimed by strangers online with extreme skepticism.
- If communication becomes urgent and financial, pause and verify before responding.

Lesson Learned

This scam works by building anticipation, then introducing crisis at the last moment. The emotional investment in an upcoming meeting makes it harder to step back and question the situation.

Final Thought: A real visit does not depend on emergency payments or sudden crises. When every step toward meeting requires sending more money, the journey is not real—it is engineered.

FINAL WORD

Regardless of how much you've read, the world of dating sites includes both positive and negative experiences.

This booklet is not written to discourage relationships or create fear, but to encourage awareness. Caution, observation, and emotional control can make a significant difference when interacting with strangers online.

Many of the stories shared here come from real experiences—some my own, and some shared by trusted friends who went through similar situations. I gathered them together with the intention of helping others avoid the same mistakes, not to generalize or label any group of people.

It is also important to clarify that these experiences are not limited to one gender or one type of person. While I have written from what I personally went through and observed, similar situations can involve anyone, regardless of gender or background. The focus here is the pattern of behavior, not the identity of the individual.

If your goal is a serious relationship, patience is essential. Genuine connections take time to develop and are built on consistency, honesty, and real-life verification. Asking thoughtful questions and paying attention to actions over words can help you better understand the other person's intentions.

If your intentions are different, caution is still important to ensure you are not misled or emotionally exploited. In all cases, awareness and clear boundaries are your best protection.

Do not allow yourself to become someone's source of financial support when the relationship is not real or balanced. At the same time, do not lose faith in genuine connections—just learn to recognize the difference between authenticity and manipulation.

If you found this guide useful, consider sharing it with friends or family who might benefit from it. The goal is simple: to help more people stay safe, think clearly, and build healthier connections online.

Thank you for taking the time to read this booklet.

The Author

READING AND RESOURCES

All references listed below, up to the time this booklet was written, are reliable, and their content has been verified. These references aim to confirm that the stories mentioned in this book are real and not fictional or generated by artificial intelligence. Many people have been victims of fraud and scams on dating platforms, and their real-life experiences offer us important lessons in awareness and caution.

For anyone who wishes to explore the topic of this booklet in more depth and learn about additional stories, experiences, advice, and real incidents, the reference below can be used as a guide to help you understand the risks and take the necessary precautions to protect yourself. It is always essential to verify sources and handle information carefully, as the digital world is rife with temptations and risks. Awareness is the first line of defense against scammers.

Pew Research Center. 2020. *Roughly Six-in-Ten U.S. Online Daters Are Concerned About Data Collection.*
https://www.pewresearch.org/fact-tank/2020/05/29/roughly-six-in-ten-online-daters-in-the-u-s-are-concerned-about-data-collection/

Oak, Rajvardhan, Muhammad Shafiq, and Zubair Shafiq. 2025. *"Hello, Is This Anna?: A First Look at Pig-Butchering Scams."*
https://arxiv.org/abs/2503.20821

Tinder. 2018. *Tinder Privacy Policy.*
https://policies.tinder.com/privacy-2018-5-25/intl/en/

Commodity Futures Trading Commission (CFTC). 2025. *Customer Advisory: Six Warning Signs of Online Financial Romance Frauds.*
https://www.cftc.gov/LearnAndProtect/AdvisoriesAndArticles/RomanceScam.html

ProFaceFinder. 2025. *Reverse Image Search for Scammers.*
https://profacefinder.com/reverse-image-search-scammer-photos/

Newswire. 2022. *Global Anti-Scam Alliance Survey Reveals 25% of Dating Users Report Being Scammed.*
https://www.newswire.com/news/global-anti-scam-alliance-survey-reveals-25-of-dating-users-report-21625010

Commodity Futures Trading Commission (CFTC). 2025. *"Dating or Defrauding?" A Joint Effort to Alert Online Daters and Social Media Users of Relationship Investment Scams.* https://www.cftc.gov/PressRoom/PressReleases/9052-25

Associated Press (AP). 2025. *Interpol Says 260 Suspects in Online Romance Scams Have Been Arrested in Africa.* https://apnews.com/article/85af8ffb6c257a902ce3360cabf28974

Wikipedia. 2025. *Pig Butchering Scam.* https://en.wikipedia.org/wiki/Pig_butchering_scam

Federal Trade Commission (FTC). 2024. *Does a Friend You Met Online Need Money for an Emergency? That's a Scam.* https://consumer.ftc.gov/consumer-alerts/2024/06/does-friend-you-met-online-need-money-emergency-thats-scam

Associated Press (AP). 2023. *Woman Gets Over 6 Years in Prison for Role in Romance Scams.* https://apnews.com/article/20de40b00c4fae48210ee117ec002f75

Federal Bureau of Investigation (FBI). 2025. *Romance Scams.* https://www.fbi.gov/how-we-can-help-you/scams-and-safety/common-frauds-and-scams/romance-scams

U.S. Department of Justice. 2020. *Three Charged with Conspiracy to Launder Money in an Online Romance Scam.* https://www.justice.gov/usao-sdoh/pr/three-charged-money-laundering-conspiracy-involving-online-romance-scam

U.S. Army. 2025. *The Facts About Soldiers' Meal Card Plans and Basic Allowance for Subsistence (BAS).* https://www.army.mil/article/283532/the_facts_about_soldiers_meal_card_plans_and_basic_allowance_for_subsistence_bas

THANK YOU, READER

Thank you for taking the time to read this book. Your interest, support, and engagement truly mean a great deal to me.

I hope this work has resonated with you and offered value, reflection, or insight in some way.

Your support as a reader is deeply appreciated.

NOTES

NOTES